Literacy and Language
Pupils' Book

2

Janey Pursglove and **Charlotte Raby**

Series developed by **Ruth Miskin**

OXFORD
UNIVERSITY PRESS

OXFORD
UNIVERSITY PRESS

Great Clarendon Street, Oxford, OX2 6DP,
United Kingdom

Oxford University Press is a department of the
University of Oxford. It furthers the University's
objective of excellence in research, scholarship,
and education by publishing worldwide.
Oxford is a registered trade mark of Oxford
University Press in the UK and in certain
other countries

British Library Cataloguing in Publication Data
Data available

ISBN: 978-0-19-833067-7

10 9 8 7 6 5 4 3

Paper used in the production of this book is a
natural, recyclable product made from wood grown
in sustainable forests. The manufacturing process
conforms to the environmental regulations of the
country of origin.

Printed in China by Imago

Acknowledgements

Cover illustration by Tony Ross

Illustrations by: Laura Anderson; Galia Bernstein;
Leo Broadley; Margaret Chamberlain; Ester Garcia
Cortes; Violeta Dabija; Anais Goldemberg; Alexandra
Huard; Meg Hunt; Constanze Von Kitzing; Sole Otero;
Q2A; Andrés Martínez Ricci; Yannick Robert;
Tony Ross; Lily Trotter; Bee Willey

The publishers would like to thank the following for
permission to reproduce images: **p9l**: Paul Hakimata
Photography/Shutterstock; **p9r**: Micha Klootwijk/
Shutterstock; **p11**: Gertjan Hooijer/Shutterstock; **p12**:
roundstripe/Shutterstock; **p12** clockwise from top: Ian
Grainger/Shutterstock; dabjola/iStock; DanielaAgius/
iStock; Eric Isselée/Shutterstock; Antagain/iStock;
p13: clearviewstock/Shutterstock; **p14–15**: Tischenko
Irina/Shutterstock; **p17t**: R-studio/Shutterstock; **p17b**:
Anky/Shutterstock; **p18tl**: konmesa/Shutterstock;
p18tr: Stu Porter/Shutterstock; **p18bl**: Mogens Trolle/
Shutterstock; **p18br**: Peter Betts/Shutterstock; **p19**:
Dobermaraner/Shutterstock; p20: Africa Studio/
Shutterstock; **p21** clockwise from top: Anna segeren/
Shutterstock; Elr.Sanchez/Shutterstock; stephan
kerkhofs/Shutterstock; Tyler Fox/Shutterstock;
Lawrence Cruciana/Shutterstock; Cigdem Sean
Cooper/Shutterstock; **p22**: RCB Shooter/Shutterstock;
p33 clockwise from top: hehe/Shutterstock; LenLis/
Shutterstock; PinkPueblo/Shutterstock; **p42t**: A-R-T/
Shutterstock; **p42b**: primeproud/Shutterstock; **p44**:
Sophia Matthew/OUP; **p50**: Volkova/Shutterstock;
p60: Triff/Shutterstock; **p61t**: Volodymyr Burdiak/
Shutterstock; **p61b**: Atlaspix/Shutterstock; **p62**:
Artspace/Shutterstock; **p63t**: Transia_art/Shutterstock;
p63b: Yai/Shutterstock

TEACHERS:
For inspirational support plus
free resources and eBooks
www.oxfordprimary.co.uk

PARENTS:
Help your child's learning
with essential tips, phonics
support and free eBooks
www.oxfordowl.co.uk

Contents

Sister FOR SALE

Reading

 **1 Secret story 3**

Discuss the questions.

A Do you think Molly is a good big sister?

B How would *you* feel if someone treated you like a baby?

C What do you think will happen to Tom at school now?

② Class log

Discuss the questions.

Tom

★ What is Tom like?

★ How does he feel about Molly?

★ How does he feel about Rory?

Rory

★ What is Rory like?

★ How does he feel about Tom?

★ How do you think he feels after Molly stands up to him?

③ Grammar: capital letters

Take turns to read the sentences. Discuss which words should have capital letters.

A on friday, tom's big sister, molly, met him outside the school gates.

B tom's favourite sweet shop is called tasty treats.

④ Role-play

Partner 1 is the Agony Aunt and asks the questions. Partner 2 is Molly and answers the questions.

★ Can you describe the problems you are having with your little brother?

★ What do you do for him?

★ How do you feel when he gets cross with you?

★ Why do you think Tom doesn't like you helping him?

★ What do you think you can do to sort the problem out?

1 What if not...?

Discuss these What if not...? questions.

A What if not *an enemy?* What if Rory, the bully, were *Tom's friend?*

B What if not *mummying?* What if Molly *embarrassed Tom in another way?*

C What if not *younger?* What if Tom were the *older sibling?*

2 Write a story 1

Read and discuss these Top Tips for planning your story.

★ Just include the key points.

★ Imagine where parts of your story could take place in your school.

★ Think about how each character will react.

★ Re-read your plan to your partner. Does it make sense? Have you missed out anything important?

③ Grammar: suffixes

Take turns to read each column in the table below.

Root word	pain	care	hope	use
+ -ful suffix	painful	careful	hopeful	useful
+ -less suffix	painless	careless	hopeless	useless

Choose a column and make three sentences using each of the words. Write your sentences in your Personal log.

④ Personal log

Read the prompts and Special phrases with your partner. Use them to help you write your story opening.

Prompts

★ Introduce the big brother or sister in your story.

★ Explain what the problem is.

★ Give an example of how they embarrassed you at home or at school.

Special phrases

It all started…   Every day…   Until then…

From that moment on…   It began with…

① Zoom in on explanations

Take turns to read the list of key features. How many examples can you find in 'Parents and their Young'?

Key features

★ an introduction

★ conjunctions (e.g. *and, because, but, until, so, if*)

★ adverbs of time (e.g. *first, meanwhile, finally, then*)

★ technical language

★ questions

② Write 2

Choose some adverbs of time and conjunctions to improve your paragraph. Discuss your changes before writing them in your Personal log.

Adverbs of time

first   meanwhile   finally   then   next

Conjunctions

...**and** can produce up to 1,000 eggs in an hour.

...**so** they can chase small insects to eat.

...**because** they have legs like a frog.

③ Write 3

Take turns to read these notes. Use some of them to add extra information to your life cycle.

- frogs – eggs in shallow water (ponds, streams)

- lots of eggs – many won't survive

- white jelly protects eggs – tadpoles eat it when they hatch

- tadpoles hatch – 6 to 21 days

- grow teeth 4 weeks later

- grow legs and arms 6 to 9 weeks after birth

- froglets – stumpy tails which disappear

- froglets grow into adults – 12 to 16 weeks from birth

- winter – frogs hibernate

- spring – frogs return to pond to mate

④ Evaluate and edit

Read the evaluation points below with your partner.

My frog life cycle:

★ gives information about the key stages in a frog's life

★ uses technical language to give the reader information about frogs.

Grammar:

★ includes conjunctions to link ideas in the same sentence

★ includes adverbs of time to structure the text clearly.

Discuss how well Partner 1's writing has included the points. Then do the same for Partner 2's writing.

Poetry

Reading

1 Wishes and consequences

Discuss the questions.

What will you wish for?

★ Will you change something about yourself or someone else?

★ Will you wish for a super power?

★ Will you wish for something you have been trying to save up for?

What will happen when you make your wish?

★ How will you change?

★ What could go wrong?

★ Could anyone get hurt?

② **Class log**

Discuss which cover design you think is the best and why.

A

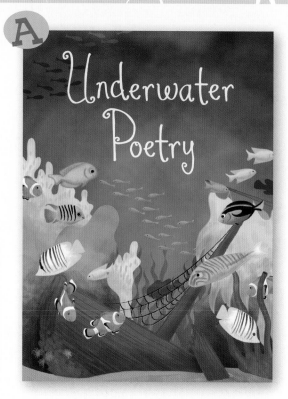

B

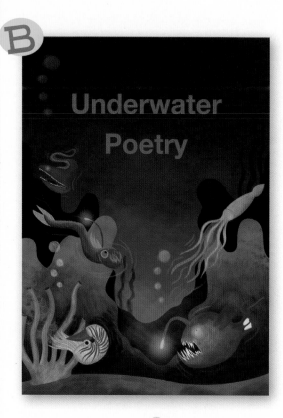

C

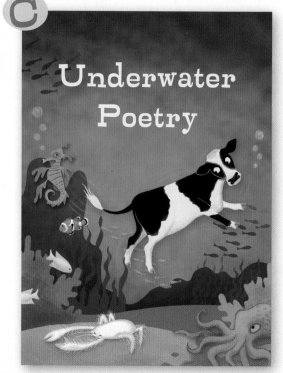

③ Think and link 2

Take it in turns to read these words. Use some of them to create kennings to describe the car and the castle that the fish wished for.

Word bank

guzzler giant tall

fast palace grand speedy

quick expensive runner

home King's treasure

holder keeper noisy crown

stone brick metal

enormous posh tower speeder

4 Discuss a performance

Think about your own performance and discuss the questions.

★ How did you emphasise the rhyme and repetition in your performance?

★ How did you use actions?

★ How did you divide up the lines in the poem?

Now choose one of the other performances and discuss the questions.

★ What pictures did you see in your head when you were listening to the other group perform?

★ What did you enjoy about the performance?

★ How did the performers emphasise the rhyme and repetition in their performance?

★ What actions did they use?

Writing

① Grammar: commas in lists

Read Peter's note. He put the commas in the wrong places. Discuss where he should have put the commas.

> Hi Mum
> I need to get some shopping but I'm too busy writing poems. Please could you go to the shops for me?
> I need a lemon hamster, food, mouse, mat for my computer, paper socks, tie eraser and biscuits.
> Thanks
> Peter

② What if not...?

Read the What if not…? question.

What if not *a sea creature?* What if there were *a wildlife park under the sea?*

Think of some animals you might find at a wildlife park. Discuss how they would survive under water.

★ Where would the animals live?

★ How would they move under water?

★ What would they eat?

③ Word play 1

Take turns to choose an animal to describe. Pick one word from box A and one from box B to create a kenning. Write your kennings in your Personal log.

 A

What it looks like:

grey	ferocious
hairy	stripy
proud	giant

 B

How it moves:

plodder	springer
jumper	speeder
pouncer	strider

④ Write a poem 1

Discuss the questions.

★ What colour is your creature? What texture is its skin/fur?

★ Does your creature hunt or is it hunted?

★ What is your creature's favourite food?

★ Where does your creature sleep at night?

⑤ Write a poem 3

Discuss these Top Tips for ordering your poem.

★ Read each kenning aloud before you decide where it should go.

★ Create rhyming pairs where possible.

★ Read each part of the poem aloud to see if it creates a good rhythm.

★ Think about the shape of your poem.

⑥ Evaluate and edit

Read the evaluation points below with your partner.

My poem:

★ includes interesting information about my new sea creature, such as where it lives or what it eats

★ uses at least one poetic technique, e.g. *rhyme, rhythm, repetition* and *alliteration*

★ includes kennings arranged in an interesting shape.

Grammar:

★ includes commas to tell the reader when to pause.

Discuss how well Partner 1's writing has included the points. Then do the same for Partner 2's writing.

① Questions

Discuss the photos. Think of some questions about shipwrecks and the kind of creatures that might live in them.

② Grammar: suffixes 2 -er and -est

Make up sentences using these words. Say them aloud before writing them in your Personal log.

deep	deeper	deepest
dark	darker	darkest
quick	quicker	quickest

③ Evaluate and edit

Read the evaluation points below with your partner.

My text about shipwrecks:

★ uses features like *headings*, *subheadings* and *pictures* to make it easy for the reader to find information

★ includes interesting information from my notes

★ includes facts, not opinions.

Grammar:

★ includes correct use of -er and -est suffixes if comparisons are made.

Discuss how well Partner 1's writing has included the points. Then do the same for Partner 2's writing.

Oh, Gnome!

Reading

(1) Secret script 3

Discuss the questions.

A Why did Oliver disobey Gran?

B Was Katie right to say they had to tell the truth?

C Who did you feel most sorry for –
Oliver, Katie, Jerome or Gran? Why?

② **Class log**

Discuss which poster is the best advert for the play and why.

A

Oh, Gnome!
a play by Lou Kuenzler
Denton Community Hall
Saturday, 3 March – 2.30 p.m.

Tickets – Children £2
Adults £3.50

"We loved Jerome the gnome!
A 'must see' play!" Denton Daily

B

★ **Oh , Gnome!** ★
a play by **Lou Kuenzler**

Denton
Community Hall
Saturday, 3 March
2.30 p.m.

TICKETS
Children £2
Adults £3.50

"We loved Jerome
the gnome!
A 'must see' play!"
Denton Daily

C

Oh, Gnome!
a play by Lou Kuenzler

Denton Community Hall
Saturday, 3 March — 2.30 p.m.
Tickets — Children £2
Adults £3.50

"We loved Jerome the gnome!
A 'must see' play!"
Denton Daily

3 Grammar: sentences with different forms

If you *command* someone to do something, you *tell* them to do it quite forcefully.

Take turns to read the sentences below. Decide which ones are commands.

A That cake tastes disgusting!

B Do you know where my socks are?

C Sit down and do your homework.

D Put that down, right now!

E I think the house is haunted!

4 Personal log

Discuss which part of the play the pictures show.

Choose a character from one of the pictures. Tell your partner what you would be saying and thinking if you were that character.

⑤ Who's the most important?

Take turns to read the text below. Discuss who you think the most important character is and why.

Katie   We'll be really careful...

Gran   Wait until after lunch. We'll go to the shops and buy a soft ball to use. There's pizza in the oven. It'll only take a few minutes. *(She goes back into the house.)*

Oliver   *(Whispering)* Just let me bowl once, Katie. There's a spin shot I really want to try.

Katie and Jerome   *(Together)* Grandma said no!

What's the most important moment in the play?

Discuss which of these statements you agree with the most and why.

The most important moment of the play is…

A When Oliver finds the old cricket bat and ball in the garage. If he hadn't found those, they wouldn't have broken Jerome!

B When Gran goes inside to check on the pizza. If she had stayed in the garden, the twins would not have disobeyed her.

C When Jerome gets broken. That is what caused the trouble and upset Gran.

D When Katie and Oliver tell Gran the truth. They would have lost her trust if they had lied to her.

27

Writing

① Write a script 1

Take turns to read the prompts and choose one to use in your role-play.

Oliver feels…

★ Glad, because he never liked that grumpy looking gnome.

★ Guilty, because he broke Jerome.

★ Sad, because he always liked Jerome and will miss seeing him when he visits Gran.

★ Excited about Gran taking Jerome to a car boot sale because he has some old toys he would like to sell.

② Build a script 2

Take turns to play the role of Jerome and answer a hotseat question.

★ On your way to the car boot sale this morning, what were you thinking about?

★ What sort of new home would you like to go to?

★ Who do you blame for the fact that you are being sold? Why?

★ What will happen if nobody buys you?

★ Would you like to stay with Grandma or are you looking forward to living with a new family?

③ Write a script 3

Take turns to read the notes for a new ending below. Then use the prompts to help you write your script.

- Jerome fell in love with Bluebell the fairy when they were on the shelf at the garden centre.
- Jerome saw Bluebell on another table at the car boot sale.
- Jerome and Bluebell were bought by the same family.
- They went to live a new life together.

Prompts

★ Think about how amazed and excited Jerome is when he spots Bluebell.

★ What will Bluebell say or think when she sees Jerome?

★ Where are they taken to live? Are they happy? What do they say?

What would Jerome prefer?

Here are notes for a different ending. Read them and discuss which ending Jerome would like best.

- Katie and Oliver ask what's happened to Jerome. All Grandma will say is that he has gone to a good home.
- Oliver helps to pack up at the end of the day.
- They get back to Grandma's house and Grandma pulls Jerome out of her bag.
- Katie and Oliver are very surprised.
- Grandma says that this is the good home and she is using the money she made at the car boot sale to buy Jerome a little pond all of his own.
- Katie and Oliver are thrilled and promise to help look after the pond and Jerome.

① Role-play

Partner 1 is Rosie.　　Partner 2 is Adam.

Try to use some of the phrases below to help you create your role-play.

> Oh, go on…
>
> No one will know…
>
> Yes, but you…
>
> As your friend, I think…
>
> It wouldn't be fair because…

② Grammar: adjectives and nouns

Look at the sentence below. The adjective and the noun have been underlined.

Take off those <u>filthy</u> <u>boots</u>.

Take turns to read these sentences. Identify the adjectives and nouns.

A　Emma rode a silver bike.

B　Look at that battered, old skateboard.

C　Why not have some delicious, warm pizza?

③ Write 1

Use the words and phrases below to help you make a poster to advertise the table-top sale.

★ Stalls will sell children's books, bags of sweets, toys and home-made cakes.

★ The sale will take place after school.

★ It will cost 50p.

★ The sale will be held in the school hall.

Word bank

bargain	sale	tasty	fun
brilliant	delicious	value	treats

Phrases bank

Don't miss it!	Come and buy!
Only 50p!	One day only!

4 Write 2

Use these Top Tips to help you create a fantastic leaflet.

★ Keep it simple – don't use too many words.

★ Think about what the reader *needs* to know.

★ Use pictures to engage and interest your reader.

★ Use boxes to make the information stand out.

5 Write 3

With your partner, choose the best voice-over lines to match each storyboard square on page 35.

A It started as a game. It became a matter of life or death…

B Coming soon to a 3D cinema near you!

C Meet Jerome the gnome. How could he have guessed his quiet life was about to change forever?

D Is this a new beginning, or the end for Jerome?

E Can Grandma's love save him from disaster?

F Someone's broken more than a promise…

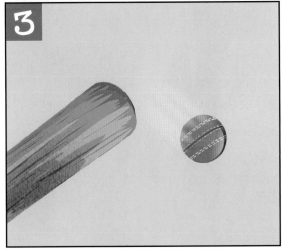

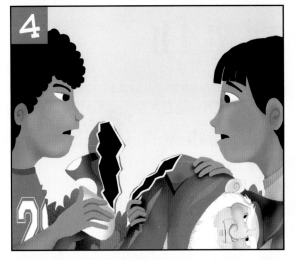

Beauty and the Beast

Reading

1 **Secret story 3**

Discuss the questions.

A What do you think the Beast wanted?

B Was Beauty's father wrong to pick one of the Beast's roses?

C Why do you think Beauty grew to love the Beast?

D Which character is your favourite? Why?

② Grammar: conjunctions

Take turns to read the sentences. Discuss which conjunction you would choose in each sentence.

A Beauty's father begged the Beast to change his mind **and/but/or** he would not listen.

B Beauty had to decide whether to stay with the Beast **and/but/or** go home to see her sick father.

C The Beast was in love with Beauty **and/but/or** he wanted to marry her.

③ What if not...?

Discuss these What if not…? questions.

A What if not *a rose?* What if Beauty had asked for *clothes like her sister?*

B What if not *a good daughter?* What if Beauty had *not gone to live with the Beast in her father's place?*

C What if not *a handsome prince?* What if the Beast had turned into *a frog* when Beauty kissed him?

1 Write a story 1

Play the Story maker game.

Characters

frog

princess

giant

wicked witch

wolf

beast

Settings

1 mountain

2 beautiful garden

3 woods

4 cottage

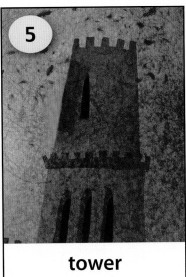

5 tower

6 castle

② Personal log

Take turns to read the words. Then choose two or three words to describe your character.

kind   pretty   happy   rich

caring   huge   brave   popular

cruel   ugly   sad   poor

selfish   small   cowardly   lonely

Now choose two or three words to describe your setting.

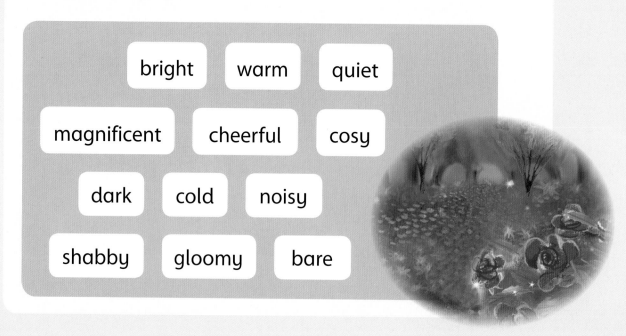

bright   warm   quiet

magnificent   cheerful   cosy

dark   cold   noisy

shabby   gloomy   bare

③ Write a story 2

Read the prompts and discuss what your character wants.

Prompts

My character wants:

★ to find someone or something that has been lost

★ to change or transform someone or something

★ to be rich

★ to have someone to love.

Choose a Special phrase. Use it to write a sentence about what your character wants.

Special phrases

There was nothing else he wanted, just…

All he ever wanted was…

Her heart's desire was…

She had just one wish, to…

1 Instruction detectives

Match the headings to the instruction texts A, B or C.

Headings

★ Grow a Beanstalk of Your Own

★ Rules of the Countryside

★ Watch out! Thieves about!

B

★ Be safe, plan ahead and follow the signs.

★ Leave gates and property as you find them.

★ Take your rubbish home.

★ Keep dogs under control.

A

Lock your things away

1 Place items in a locker.

2 Put money in.

3 Turn key to lock.

C

1 First of all, carefully make a small hole in the soil.

2 Next, gently place one seed in the hole.

3 Cover with soil and pat firmly.

4 Finally, sprinkle with water.

② Grammar: adverbs 1

Read these silly sentences. Look at the adverbs of manner in bold. Swap them between the sentences to make sensible sentences.

A Talk **loudly** if you don't want to be overheard.

B You will need to run **slowly** if you want to catch the bus.

C The thunder rumbled extremely **quietly**.

D My brother opened his present so **quickly**, I had to ask him to hurry up.

③ Write 1

Discuss the activities below. Then choose one to mime.

A Wrapping a present.

B Feeding a cat or dog.

C Getting ready for bed.

D Cleaning a bike.

④ Write 3

Discuss the pictures. Use them to help you write your own set of instructions.

Chatterbox Ben

Reading

(1) Secret story 3

Discuss the questions.

A Was it fair that Ben had to stay in at break for talking during a spelling test?

B What do you think would have happened if Ben hadn't lost his voice?

C What do you think the other children in the class think about Ben?

② What if not...?

Discuss these What if not...? questions.

A What if not *a Sponsored Silence?* What if Class 2J did *a Sponsored Talk?*

B What if not *a chatterbox?* What if Ben were like Eric in The Night Shimmy *and didn't like talking?*

C What if not *Ben talking?* What if he had *an invisible friend who spoke for him?*

③ Find it or prove it

Discuss the questions. Find evidence in the text to support your answers.

A Who tries hard not to sneeze during the Sponsored Silence practice?

B How do we know that Miss Johnson is irritated when Ben explains why he is late?

C Who will Miss Johnson choose to tell everyone about the zoo if they win the reward?

Writing

① Character detectives

Discuss the questions.

A Did you feel sorry for Marcia? Why?

B Would you like to have a friend like Marcia? Why?

C Which three words would you choose to describe Marcia?

gentle   mysterious   thoughtful   cheerful

playful   kind   understanding   funny

② Grammar: conjunctions

Take turns to read the sentences. Discuss which conjunction you would choose in each sentence.

A Children called Eric names **that/when** he wouldn't speak.

B The Night Shimmy helped Eric **if/that** he had bad dreams.

C Perhaps Eric didn't like talking **because/that** he was shy.

D Eric was glad **that/if** Marcia became his friend.

③ **Dramatic reconstruction**

Partner 1 is Ben.
Partner 2 is Ben's invisible friend.

Use the story squares to plan and practise your role-play. Think about:

★ how the characters will stand or move

★ what the characters will say

★ what the characters' facial expressions will be like.

④ Write a story 3

Write a diary entry about how the goal is saved. You should begin your entry as it is written below, and choose one of the words to fill in the gap.

Dear Diary,
What a .... day this has been!

brilliant	fantastic	great	superb

jaw-dropping	stunning	wonderful

Now use the prompts to help you write the rest of your diary entry.

Prompts

★ Write as if you are Ben talking to himself. Use the first person *I, my* and *me*.

★ Write in the past tense. Ben is writing about things that have already happened.

1 Say it

Read Miss Dixon's diary entry.

Wednesday, 29 May

Must mark spelling tests by tomorrow!

Need to plan the class fair!

Ideas so far:

- need a mix of stalls — things to sell and games to play
- organise letters home, adverts, tickets, etc.

Check how much we can spend and sort out prizes.

Choose a date for the fair — need to check when the school hall is free!

Just remembered — Mum's birthday tomorrow.

Take card and flowers after school!

Now use the prompts to discuss how she feels about the class fair.

Prompts

★ How can you tell that Miss Dixon has a lot to do?

★ Why do you think there are so many exclamation marks?

★ Choose some words to describe how Miss Dixon is feeling:

worried	excited	pleased	delighted
scared	anxious	annoyed	relaxed
rushed	pressured	enthusiastic	

② Write 1

Take turns to read the diary notes below.
Then use them to help you write an email to
the staff at Denton Dale Primary School.

Thursday, 6 June

- Send an email to all staff.
- Tell them you have booked the school hall for Friday, 21 June from 9 a.m. until 6 p.m.
- Ask for help on the day of the fair.
- Ask for donations of prizes for stalls.
- Ask for suggestions of ideas for stalls.
- Let them know that more details will be sent later.

③ Write 2

Use the table and the prompts below it to help you write an invitation.

Who is the invitation for?	Friends and family
Reason for writing	Class fair to raise money for outdoor play equipment
Details	• crafts for sale • games and prizes • snacks
When is it?	• Friday, 21 June • 3.30–6 p.m.
Where is it?	Main Hall, Denton Dale Primary School, Brick Road, Denton

Prompts

★ Your invitation can be *informal* and *chatty*.

★ Make sure the information is clear and easy to read.

4 **Grammar: apostrophes for contractions**

Take turns to read the sentences below. Discuss which ones you would use in:

★ a *formal* piece of writing

★ an *informal* chat with a friend.

A We've worked hard on this project.

B We have worked hard on this project.

C You must not leave before it is finished.

D You mustn't leave before it's finished.

E I didn't expect so many people to come.

F I did not expect so many people to come.

5 **Write 3**

Partner 1 is Mr Hartley.
Partner 2 is Mrs Sharp.

Plan and practise your role-play. Think about:

★ what you will say and how you will say it

★ whether you will show your feelings on your face

★ whether you will keep calm or get cross

★ whether Mr Hartley will get a refund.

Chocolate Planet

Reading

① **Secret story 3**

Discuss the questions.

A Was it fair of Gala and Frag to trick the moondog so they could get the chocolate?

B Why do you think Gala and Frag went back to Planet Wob if it was such a boring place?

C Would *you* have been brave enough to face the moondog? What would you have done if you were Gala or Frag?

② Find it or prove it

TTYP

Discuss the questions. Find evidence in the text to support your answers.

A Why is Planet Wob dull?

B Why does Frag say that Gala shouldn't have bothered packing the turnips?

C What does the moondog look like?

D What happens to the moondog at the end of the story?

③ What if not...?

Discuss these What if not…? questions.

A What if not *dull?* What if Planet Wob were *exciting and full of scrumptious things to eat?*

B What if not *a two-headed moondog monster?* What if the moondog were *a cute moondog puppy?*

C What if not *a fantasy story set in space?* What if the story had *a realistic setting?*

④ Grammar: verb tenses

Take turns to read the columns in the table below.

Present tense	landing	walking	stepping	glowing
Past tense	landed	walked	stepped	glowed

Choose one present tense verb and one past tense verb. Take turns to make up two sentences using the verbs.

Writing

① Multi-syllabic words

Take turns to read the words and synonyms. Choose at least two words each and build a sentence for each one.

> *ferocious* – fearsome, fierce, savage

> *precious* – valuable, treasured

> *scrumptious* – yummy, mouth-watering, delicious

> *imagination* – thoughts, ideas, pictures in your head

② What if not...?

Discuss this What if not...? question. Use the pictures on page 59 to help you.

What if not the *Chocolate Planet?* What if Gala and Frag decided to visit *a different planet?*

What if *Planet Precious?*

What if *Planet Party?*

③ Grammar: tenses in texts

Take turns to read the sentences.

A As the astronauts are walking through the space station, they are chatting about their next mission.

B As the astronauts walked through the space station, they chatted about their next mission.

Discuss which sentence is written in the present tense and which is written in the past tense.

④ Story talk

Discuss the final parts of your story.

The problem

★ Who or what is stopping Gala and Frag from getting what they want?

★ What does it look like?

★ What does it sound like?

Gala and Frag overcome the problem by:

★ playing a trick   ★ using magic

★ being brave   ★ being clever.

① Presenting information

Match the headings to the information texts A, B or C. Then discuss how each one is presented.

Headings

★ Weather forecast

★ Menu

★ Encyclopaedia entry

A

Tigers belong to the cat family. They are one of the largest species of wild cats.

B

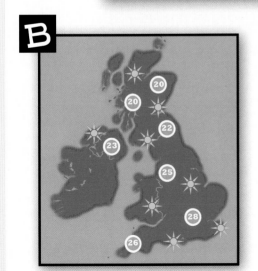

C

Starters
Soup of the day
Garlic mushrooms

Mains
Chicken and mushroom pie
Vegetable lasagne

② **Write 2**
TTYP

Partner 1 look at A.   Partner 2 look at B.

Use the information to fill in your Chocolate Fact File.

A

Rocky Raider

Only 65p

Suitable for vegetarians
Ingredients:
Syrup, Dried milk, Sugar, Vegetable fat, Cocoa, Colourings, Flavourings – caramel and toffee

Nutrition	Per bar	GDA Children 5–10 years
Calories	210 kcal	1800 kcal
Fat	7g	70g
Sugars	33g	85g
Protein	1g	24g

Made in England

B

Nutty Nuggets

Contains nuts

Store in a cool place
Ingredients:
Milk, Sugar, Butterfat, Cocoa, Colourings, Flavourings – cherry and hazelnut

Nutrition	Per bar	GDA Children 5–10 years
Calories	190 kcal	1800 kcal
Fat	11g	70g
Sugars	27g	85g
Protein	3g	24g

③ **Write 3**

Take turns to read sections of the web page below. Then use the information to make notes on the Mayas.

The Mayas

The Mayas loved their cocoa! They made a frothy chocolate drink with it called xocolatl, meaning 'bitter water'.

Cocoa beans weren't just used to make this delicious drink. The Mayas were brilliant at maths and often spread cocoa beans on the ground and used them as counters.

The Mayas also used cocoa beans as money. Merchants would travel by canoe to swap the beans for cloth and feathers that they would use to make their wonderful clothes.

④ Evaluate

Read the evaluation points below with your partner.

Our chocolate exhibition:

★ presents information in a variety of ways, e.g. *photos, quiz questions, fact files, pictures*

★ includes an accordion booklet.

Grammar:

★ uses capital letters for names of things or places.

Discuss how well your exhibition has included the points.

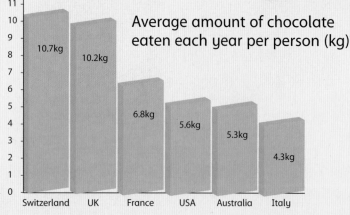

Average amount of chocolate eaten each year per person (kg)

Switzerland 10.7kg
UK 10.2kg
France 6.8kg
USA 5.6kg
Australia 5.3kg
Italy 4.3kg